CW00322151

101 DYNAM[IC IDEAS]
FOR YOUR
YOUTH GROUP

Other titles by Andy Back:

Acts of God: The Storyline
Dan the Man: The Storyline

101 DYNAMIC IDEAS – FOR YOUR YOUTH GROUP

ANDY BACK

WORD PUBLISHING
Word (UK) Ltd
Milton Keynes, England
WORD AUSTRALIA
Kilsyth, Victoria, Australia
WORD COMMUNICATIONS LTD
Vancouver, B.C., Canada
STRUIK CHRISTIAN BOOKS (PTY) LTD
Maitland, South Africa
ALBY COMMERCIAL ENTERPRISES PTE LTD
Balmoral Road, Singapore
CHRISTIAN MARKETING NEW ZEALAND LTD
Havelock North, New Zealand
JENSCO LTD
Hong Kong
SALVATION BOOK CENTRE
Malaysia

101 DYNAMIC IDEAS FOR YOUR YOUTH GROUP

© 1991 Andy Back

Published in the UK by Word (UK) Ltd./Frontier Publishing International

All rights reserved

No part of this publication may be reproduced or transmitted in any form or by any means, electronic or mechanical, including photocopy, recording or any information storage or retrieval system, without permission in writing from the publishers.

ISBN 0-85009-702-9 (Australia ISBN 1-86258-166-5)

Reproduced, printed and bound in Great Britain for Word (UK) Ltd. by Richard Clay Ltd.,Bungay.

91 92 93 94 / 10 9 8 7 6 5 4 3 2 1

ACKNOWLEDGEMENTS

There is no way that this book could have been written without the contribution of past and present members of the team with whom I work at Dunamis. I especially want to thank Chris and Debbie Jarvis for teaching me many of the principles and activities contained within these pages.

To
James Bloice-Smith
an evangelist, friend and fellow youth leader,
who demonstrated to me that young people
will more readily receive the words we preach
when we minister to the whole person

Frontier Publishing International is committed to the production of printed and recorded materials with the view to reaching this generation with the gospel of the kingdom. FPI is part of New Frontiers International, a team ministry led by Terry Virgo, which is involved in planting and equipping churches according to New Testament principles. New Frontiers International is also responsible for a wide range of training programmes and conferences.

CONTENTS

INTRO

I have been working with teenagers on a regular basis for more than five years, in the youth group for 11-14s based at Clarendon Church, Brighton (Hove, actually). Having a name for the group gives the young people a sense of identity and belonging. The name *Dunamis* (the Greek word for power) was chosen to reflect our aim to see young people filled with the power of God, and to have a dynamic youth group to which they can invite their friends.

We make a point of giving our events titles which underline the group name. This helps both momentum and identity. Therefore we have such events as Mr Dunamight, the DunaDecathlon, The Great Dunamis Chip Shop Survey ... and constantly promote a sense of belonging. I recommend you try this with your youth group, since creative thought is good for the arteries, and can give you a laugh.

I have found that young people can be a constant source of surprise, encouragement, fun, laughter, disappointment, worry, delight, energy and wit.

The best way to serve young people is to minister to the whole person – their body, mind, emotions and social needs as well as their spiritual needs. This keeps me well away from the danger of providing just Bible classes and prayer meetings, although the Power Hour (the worship and teaching part of the evening) forms a vital part of the activities of the youth group.

In all these ideas, please remember that we have a team of trained and envisioned adults, willing to serve God in mundane practical things (like litter-picking) as well as in prayer times or ministering to young people. We believe that there is little point in running a good youth club; we aim to run the best youth club that we can, and one which is clearly identifiable as a Christian youth group. We can best serve the young people by providing excellent activities in an environment where there is good supervision, and when planning ahead, we try to remember that variety is the spice of life.

Not all of our team members are gifted in taking an up-front role – some are currently being trained and encouraged in their ministries to preach or lead worship – but each of us has to get involved with some of the mundane tasks: greeting young people as they arrive; taking the register and welcoming newcomers; refereeing the football; supervising the table-tennis and snooker; running the tuck shop; floating (which means keeping an eye on loners, discouraging fooling about in the corridors or in the toilets); or running a workshop.

TEAM SPORTS

Team games build reliance on one another, respect for the referee, obedience to the rules, and principles of encouragement and perseverance. Team sports can teach these things more quickly and effectively than a whole series of Bible studies. Doing is a better learning method than hearing, and these games are probably much more fun than the average Bible study!

The picking of teams can be a highly destructive event for those who get left until last. It's great for the good players, but what about the less able young people who want to play? The disappointment of being left out until there is no other choice can undermine all the good work of building up self-esteem done during the so-called "spiritual" time of the meeting.

Other team selection methods worth trying: appoint no-hopers as captains; instruct the captains to pick good players and poorer players alternately; invite the young people to form teams of their own choosing, but allow the no-hopers to have more players, or even allow adults to play with them. We have found that teams with adults must have some handicapping factor to redress the balance – either starting one goal down, or only allowing weaker players to be supplemented by adults.

Many youth groups play team games without a ref, which can lead to tension and arguments. We have established that a ref can dispel bad feeling by making a decision. Right or wrong, the ref's word stands. Arm the ref with a whistle, and teach the youngsters to play to the whistle, and not simply to assume a goal is awarded or whatever. It is only sensible to teach your group to play to the rules and to the whistle, so that when they enter competitions with other groups, they know how to behave.

What about taking a lesson from the world of Association Football, getting two bits of card, coloured yellow and red, and giving players of any kind of team game a reason to stay within the rules? We have found that the appearance of a yellow card can help a young person play with less aggression, when they are (as the rules allow) threatened with being sent off. And let's show young people who think they can cheat and get away with it that they cannot, and that we mean it when we apply the rules. Once a referee has sent a few players off over a period of weeks, the young people know he means business, and will play fair, with control, so that everyone will have a more enjoyable game.

The time will come when you may arrange tournaments and matches against other youth groups. Please make sure you continue to communicate wholesome values even when rules imposed by other authorities differ from yours.

1   Football

Why begin with football? Surely everyone knows how to play football, and even if they don't, then the young people in their youth group will know. But there is much more to successful football than meets the eye.

Due to lack of adequate space, teams of three players is all we can manage. True, there is room for five-a-side, but there is no room to play – there are too many tackles coming in from all sides. We may allow three minutes per game, or, on other weeks, have a one-goal-and-winners-stay-on arrangement, where a successful side are eventually beaten by fatigue, which is satisfying.

We often have knockout competitions, the most successful of which was our own World Cup, where teams were allowed to name themselves after footballing countries. There were preliminary and qualifying rounds, followed the next week by quarter-finals, semi-finals played over two legs, and then the third place match and the final itself. As with many of our larger competitions, we gave winners' medals to each player in the successful team (purchased from a local engraving and trophy shop for less than a fiver, but imparting an enormous amount of kudos to the young people). Medals and cups are awarded at the prestigious Dunawards ceremony in front of admiring parents.

2   Netball

Equipment may be a problem here. Try standing one young person on a chair at each end, and if they successfully catch the ball when goal shooters throw it to them, then a goal is awarded. Mixed teams can be fun, since the men try to take steps when holding the ball, and young women play this game vastly better than young men. It is also a good game for encouraging others to spectate. I remember many a happy hour on the touchline yelling "Windmills!"; the reason now escapes me.

Again, the same ideas about the quality and impartiality of refereeing apply.

3   Volleyball

The most important factor here is confident refereeing, due to the zany rules about rotation and only scoring on service, like badminton.

A variation on volleyball for the less ambitious is to allow the ball to bounce on each side during a rally. If the ball bounces twice, the rally is over. If the young people become too skilled at volleyball, use a rugby ball (very difficult to volley accurately), or, for messy fun, play with water-filled balloons. You may need to supply several of these.

4   Basketball

Young people on chairs can double for nets. This is not very popular with young people in our youth group, but could be a successful alternative to playing football all the time.

5   Single Wicket Cricket

We often play this indoors, with every player required to bat and bowl (six bowls to an over, of course). Scoring is as follows: any ball which hits a wall before bouncing scores four; balls which hit the ceiling before bouncing score six; no singles. Players can be out bowled, caught, stumped, or hit wicket. Fielders may also dismiss a batsman by catching the ball one-handed off the wall or ceiling, before the ball bounces on the floor.

6 Crocker

A combination of cricket and soccer, this is a Crusader game. This time the bowler has a rounders bat, and stands before a wicket made of three cricket stumps – two upright and the third across the top, making a square-shaped hole through which the bowler must bowl a football. The batsman prevents the ball from passing through his wicket by hitting the ball with the bat, but tip-and-run is again the rule. The batsman runs round a stump placed at square leg, not around the bowler's stump, which means that if the fielders can get the ball back to the bowler quickly, he will have a free shot at bowling the batsman out. NB: if you don't know where square leg stands, ask a cricketer.

Runs are scored according to completed journeys from the wicket, around the stump and back again. Batsmen may be out caught or bowled. If the football is hit behind the wicket, the batsman must run, but the run is not added to his score. If the bowler bowls and the ball hits any of the stumps, the batsman is not out. Batsmen can dismiss themselves: hitting their own wicket gives them half-out; to do this again would mean dismissal.

As players become accustomed to the rules, and skilful at the game, you can introduce a rule that after scoring 20 runs, a player must tip-and-run-two each time, which gives the bowler a better chance of a clear shot!

Another variation is to play with a rugby ball (the game is then called crugger). This is almost impossible, but hilarious, since it levels out players of different degrees of skill.

7   DunaGridIron

This is our version of American Football, a game famous for its many rules and regulations. We play indoors, which is not easy, and the game is more of a glorified bundle than a true sport, but never mind, eh?

I make no attempt here to explain the rules of American Football – actually, I think that for an Englishman like to me try to explain this game is like asking a Peruvian to explain the rules of Mah Jong to a Laplander, using only semaphore.

The two teams, offence and defence, line up facing each other, spread across the hall, with the ball in between (on what is termed *the line of scrimmage*).

On the word of command ("hut"), the ball is passed back between the legs of the player in the middle of the offence, to the *quarterback*. He catches it, and attempts either to throw it to a teammate who has run into an unmarked position, or to run with the ball himself. As soon as the word "hut" is uttered, the defence tries to prevent the offence from progressing.

As played on the fields of American Football stadia, this game is dangerous and painful. As played in the gym at our youth club, this game is just as exciting but safer.

If this seems unclear, just rejoice that your name is written in heaven, and watch the game for a few seasons on Channel Four. You'll catch on sooner or later.

All players are issued with a cloth (we used J-cloths), and they are required to leave at least half of the cloth hanging out of a pocket. Rather than bone-crunching tackles, all players have to do is to remove an opponent's cloth and thus eliminate them from that particular play.

The offence is required to gain ten yards, using four downs or attempts. If they succeed, they will probably be too near the far wall to have another try, so they return to the original line of scrimmage, but the referee makes a note to the effect that they have moved ten yards down the imaginary field. They try for another ten-yard gain, until they have made five such ten-yard gains, and then they are free to celebrate a touchdown. If they fail on their fourth down, the other team then becomes the offence and has a try.

Don't worry if this is hard work to start with; the new rules take a bit of getting used to!

8 Podex

I learned this game, just as I learned Crocker, with a Crusaders' Bible class I attended for many years. It's pronounced "puddecks", and is a kind of continuous cricket, played by two batsmen, two bowlers, fielders, and with a baseball or tennis ball, two wickets, and no pauses. Tip-and-run is the rule (if you hit the ball, you must run – and so must the other batsman), but if the fielders can get the ball to either bowler (one at each end) sufficiently quickly, the bowler may try to bowl the batsman out. The batsman does not need to be in his crease to hit the ball, but if he hits, they must run again. It is up to you to decide if they must first complete the run they were running when they hit the ball again, or if they can simply run from where they were when they hit the ball for the second time...

Runs are scored as in cricket, with boundaries and singles, etc. Batsmen can be out caught or bowled. The point of the game is that there are no pauses, even when a batsman is out and the next one is coming to the crease. If he doesn't hurry up, he may be bowled!

One important point: change the bowlers often, to give everyone a chance, and make sure that the bowling is such that the batsmen have something at which to hit.

OTHER
COMPETITIVE GAMES

This section contains some comments about various sports and games which are well-known. Oldies can be goodies, but they can also get a bit boring! With this in mind, here is the benefit of our Duna-experience.

9 Badminton

This is a highly aggressive and destructive game. Our group destroys two rackets each week, because some people have such a powerful follow-through on their slam shots that they try to follow-through through the floorboards, which is costly in terms of equipment. Our equipment manager has found a brilliant and cheap resource for rackets in car boot sales, where he often buys quality used items for a few pence. It's still a shame that they get broken so easily, but it's not too upsetting if they are inexpensive.

The occasional knockout tournament can sort out the players from the patters.

10 Table Tennis

The mainstay of many a youth group, this is a game ruined by vandalised bats, limp or broken nets, cheap ping-pong balls and lack of space. How many hours do players have to spend ferreting under chairs to find the ball? Is there any chance of a good game being played? Some good supervision can prevent the more expensive balls being stamped on wantonly, and they are so much better to play with (and more durable) than the cheap ones which burst asunder at the slightest provocation.

Competitive table tennis can be great to watch – and helps young people learn their five-times table as well!

11 Table Football

The damage done to table football games is disproportionate to the fun gained from them. But you can preserve the life of the table a little by having a rule to prevent spinning of the players; infringement could result in a free shot for the opposition.

Use your imagination here: try playing with one hand behind your back; or, when playing doubles, make defenders and attackers change places after every goal they score.

12 Snooker

It is a general rule which states that all small-sized snooker tables should have little plastic bits to support the nets hanging under the pockets, so that on the first occasion when someone tries to put the table away at the end of the evening, they immediately break off and render the net useless. The result of this is that all balls successfully pocketed drop onto the floor. Once there, they can then be kicked, slipped on or otherwise caused to interfere with other people who are innocently eating crisps elsewhere in the room, or attempting to play table tennis. It must be said that games can be impaired by high-velocity vermilion spheres rattling painfully against unsuspecting ankles.

So please carry your snooker tables with care, or be prepared to mend them often.

You may choose to go to town when you have a tournament, by supplying bow ties for players, and white gloves for referees, with constant (jokey) reprimands to the noisy audience.

13 Pool

Please see the general whinge under "snooker". If you haven't got a pool table, only snooker, then look again; one player can take five reds, and the other player take five colours, while they both play for the black. Simple, isn't it? Simple, aren't you, for not having worked that out earlier? Rude and abusive, aren't I?

There are many rules which can be introduced to make the game more skilful: players must name the pocket for which they are trying before they take their shot; the awarding of free shots following an opponent's foul, and so on.

14 Computer Games

Supervision is vital here, especially if your church or youth group funds have been spent on equipment. One drawback is that only one or two people can participate at a time, and this means that a member of your team of adults is tied up with only a few young people, while other team members may be supervising a much larger number.

Computers can be more worthwhile if young people bring their own machines in to the club meeting. Two young people brought their computers in and stayed with them, providing the supervision required to prevent damage (which gave them a sense of worth), as well as interacting well with other young people as rules and techniques were discussed and perfected.

15 Scalextric

We were fortunate enough to have a starter-kit given to us. There has been a growing interest in speed trials and endurance championships, which need some serious supervision, and plenty of partisan support and encouragement.

Once, when a team member was not supervising adequately , there was an impromptu see-how-far-you-can-get-the-car-to-fly-off-the-track-by-blasting-it-into-a-tight-corner competition, but this was both dangerous and slightly destructive, so it was discouraged.

16 Board Games

Chess and Draughts go down well, and simple games like Connect Four, Battleships and so on keep some of the less active, less able young people busy as they consume canned drinks and eat unhealthy snacks from the tuck shop.

A speed chess tournament generated some excitement, with ten seconds allowed for each move. There was little strategy, but the games were quickly brought to a conclusion. Suicide chess is a good game, too. Kings can be taken, just like any other piece, and the only rules are – if you can take a piece, you must, but you cannot move into a takeable position over the half-way line unless you're taking.

PANEL GAMES

We have attempted to generate the kind of audience hysteria achieved by some TV panel games and quiz shows, giving an opportunity for young people to 'let off steam' on an evening when we have only played sedate games and activities.

17 Categories

This is a game where pairs of young people are asked to name items that belong in various categories. They are given the category, and an example, and all they have to do is name the required number of other examples. They are allowed to use the named example as one of theirs. Ten points are awarded when the required number are correctly named; no points are scored if the pair makes an error or fails to name the required number. Indeed, any pair which fails to score is disqualified, and another is selected.

Category	Example
10 breeds of dog	Dalmatian
3 presidents of the USA since 1960	Reagan
8 chocolate bars	Mars bar
8 makes of car	Ford
8 solo female pop singers	Whitney Houston
8 TV soap operas	Emmerdale
4 comedy duos	Little & Large
5 films starring Harrison Ford	Blade Runner
10 athletics events at the Olympics	440m
6 types of footwear	sandals
10 types of fish	Halibut
4 American Football teams	San Francisco 49ers
6 first-class county cricket teams	Hampshire
4 manufacturers of soup	Heinz
8 hairstyles	quiff
8 names for streets	avenue
8 types of cake	fruit
6 building societies	Halifax
8 musical instruments that you blow	trumpet
8 writing implements	biro
6 makes of computer	Amstrad
6 professional snooker players	Steve Davis
4 professional darts players	John Lowe
6 characters in *EastEnders*	Dot Cotton
6 characters in *Neighbours*	Harold Bishop

18 The Tasting Testing

This involves young people in attempting to identify various food flavours while blindfolded. The kinds of taste sensations to which we subjected the participants included: mango chutney; mashed banana; garlic butter; cold tea; tandoori sauce; cold gravy; salted walnuts; powdered egg; grapefruit segments; stewed apple with soy sauce; prawn cocktail flavour crisps.

We also included one or two which were easy, but told the participants that they were eating something truly appalling:

      raspberry jam – rat's blood with sawdust in it
      honey – lard
      grapes – sheep's eyes
      sliced peaches – raw liver

It goes without saying that the young people enjoy the sense of adventure more when it's *others* that are having the adventure, so some of the more disgusting-sounding items may need to be fed to willing adults.

19 The Pop Panel

This is an entertaining way to communicate values about the kind of music young people enjoy. We usually invite a couple of special guests to sit on the panel – folk known by the young people to have an interest in music, such as worship leaders, singers, musicians – plus a couple of team members. We show a clip from *Top of the Pops* or one of the *Now That's What I Call Music* videos, and invite comment.

We make sure that we don't just declare it all to be sinful (because not all of it *is* sinful), and we try to play music which is enjoyable, so that there can be shades of opinion. The young people are eager to receive positive approval of their tastes in music, but we have sufficient respect from them that they hear us when we bring insight to the background of the musicians, themes and so on.

20 Blockbusters

An appealing game played on TV, which every young person will
have seen. Use any kind of relevant quiz material, and give away
tuck shop items as prizes. This can become a bit dull to watch, so
keep changing the teams answering the questions.

GENERAL ACTIVITIES

In all competitions, award points generously. There was once a famous quiz when I awarded 762 points for each right answer; the scorer had some quick maths to do, but when there were a lot of points at stake, the young people became much more excited.

21 Do-It-Yourself Quiz

Some Christian youth group leaders may still be using quizzes in the way Sunday School teachers have traditionally used them: a way of encouraging young people to listen to Bible stories. But we are called to minister to the whole person – body, mind and emotions, as well as spirit. Therefore, quizzes for their own sake can be a good way to help young people use their minds. Team quizzes have the added bonus of teaching good values in areas such as teamwork, dealing with disagreement, encouragement and so on.

A do-it-yourself quiz is the easiest quiz to prepare, because no preparation is required! Hoorah! The teams are given categories, and they have to invent questions for the other teams to answer. Announce the categories and instruct the teams to generate one question in each category. They must know the answer to their question, and the question must have just one answer – i.e. "name the big ship that hit an iceberg and sank in 1917" is acceptable; "name the people who died in the Titanic disaster" is not.

Choose, say, six, from these ideas for categories: Sport, Nature, Food, TV, History, Physics, the Bible, Pop Music, Facts about members of the youth group, Geography, Local History, Shopping, Literature, Films, Fashion, DIY, Transport.

Ten points for a correct answer; ten points to the team who invented the question which received a wrong answer or no answer.

22 Video Observation Quiz

Show a video and invite the young people to watch it carefully. Then ask questions about what they have seen. Questions should range in degree of difficulty. You can use any suitable material; one of our more successful attempts at this was a video recording which contained two minutes of a funny film, followed by five minutes of an advertising break. This was shown in small chunks, and questions asked after each part.

Typical questions could include: what make of petrol was advertised using a tiger? How much would four bedside cabinets cost from the self-assemble furniture shop? What image turned into a glass and a half of full cream milk? How many shots were fired by the policeman?

23 Giant Brain-Racker Quiz

This is easy to stage. Divide the young people into teams, and give them a general category – e.g. birds, or colours, or ball games. Each team has to think of as many varieties of things which belong in the category as they can (racking their brains), and they are given three minutes for this. They are then asked to declare the number of items in their list, and the team who declares the highest number then names everything on their list. This team gets ten points for each item mentioned. Then other teams are invited to declare items on their list not mentioned by the first team, and they score ten points for each item, with ten points taken off the first team's score for each item named by the second team. Other teams also declare items unique to their lists, and points are awarded to them, and removed from the first team. In subsequent rounds, the order of declaration must be changed to allow fairness to rule.

Ideas for categories: birds, colours, ball games, fast food, male pop stars, women in the Bible, mammals, paper, machines, fish, road transport, abbreviations, female pop stars, cartoon characters, round things, sounds, etc. The sky's the limit with many of these – have some categories with just a few items, like shops in the local High Street, nails, orange things, furniture, terms of endearment.

24 The Dunadecathlon

This consists of ten amazing activities all happening at one time, supervised by team members; the young people (divided into small groups) attempt one activity at a time. When some signal is given, they move on to the next event, until everyone has attempted everything.

It has to be said that many of these games are fun to play, even if not included in a Decathlon event.

The activities:

1. **Soccer Ball Control.** Count the number of headers, kicks or knee bounces each person can manage in a timed 60 seconds. One point for each successful bounce. The key word here is control.

2. **Upstairs, Downstairs.** Quite simply, this is one minute in which the competitor runs up and down stairs as many times as they can. Ten points for each journey - ie up and then down scores twenty points. However, no points are awarded for part-journeys, left incomplete when the time runs out.

3. **Basket Shooting.** Each person has 60 seconds and two balls. They have to score as many baskets into a basketball (or netball) net as they can, while others fetch the balls for them. One point per basket scored.

4. **Estimate a Minute.** Each competitor is told when to start, and they have to say "stop" loudly, when they think 60 seconds have elapsed. 100 points for perfect success; deduct two points per second for inaccuracy, either over or under.

5. **Clothes Pegs.** With a washing line suspended at shoulder height, each person must remove as many clothes pegs as they can using just one hand, without putting any pegs down and within 60 seconds. Five points per peg removed and five points are deducted for any pegs which are dropped.

6. **Memory Test.** Arrange a collection of 15-20 household items (brush, glass, book, toothpick, watch, cuddly toy, pencil sharpener, etc., etc.) on a tray and cover it with a cloth. Reveal the items for 20 seconds and cover them up again, while the competitors have 60 seconds to write down what they can remember. One point each for the first ten items; five points each for the rest.

7. **Hop It.** Each person must hop on one leg (without changing legs) from one end of the hall to the other and back as many times as they can within 30 seconds. Ten points for each length completed; no points for part-journeys.

8. **Balls in a Bucket.** Place a bucket or a waste bin about five yards away from any wall, and so that the competitors can stand five yards away and attempt to throw tennis balls into the bucket. Supply ten balls, and score ten points per ball in the bucket at the end of 45 seconds. Competitors may retrieve balls which fail to end up in the bucket, so long as they throw again from the required place.

9. **Skip It.** Give each person a rope, and award one point for each successful consecutive skip over the turning rope within a 30-second time limit. Five skips in a row scores five points. 24 skips, followed by a trip-up, followed by 23 skips scores 24 points, since it is consecutive skips you are counting, not cumulative, but you are kind enough to award the highest number achieved. Aren't you nice?

10.**Knocking Down Cans.** Each person aims at ten cans, arranged with four on the bottom row, three on top of them, two on top of them and one on top. Score two points for each can lying on its side at the end of three throws.

25 Rag Hockey

Two teams are lined up on either side of the hall, each numbered from the left, so that the people with the same number are on opposite ends of the hall. The referee calls a number, and the players thus designated rush out, grab a walking stick and proceed to propel a ball made from a sock stuffed with rags into his opponent's goal. Once a goal is scored, the players return the rag and their stick to the middle, return to their seats, and the ref calls another number (or, indeed, the same number, if he likes. Refs can do more or less what they want, within reason.)

This game may sound a bit dull, but as a young man I lost a fingernail playing this (ouch!) – so watch out for high-sticking and penalise it thoroughly.

26 Christian Scruples

This is a good game, suitable for communicating Christian principles in a fun format. Divide the young people into small discussion-size groups – you may prefer to have an adult in each discussion group to steer the young people towards godly conclusions. The idea is to give the options suggested, and to find the most appropriate response.

1. You find yourself being attracted to someone of the opposite gender in your school who is not a Christian, but very good-looking, and definitely the sort of person you would like to go out with. You get the impression that he/she is attracted to you, too. What do you do?
   - forget it
   - try and get the relationship started, hoping and praying that the person will become a Christian
   - get involved and enjoy yourself

2. In an RE/PSE lesson, your teacher asks how many in the class go to church. You and four others say you do. You are all then asked to say what your church is like. How would you describe your church?
   - in vague, general terms, e.g. we sing and there's a long talk
   - in very positive terms, e.g. I really enjoy the worship and learning about God
   - say very little
   - tell the truth, warts and all

3. Your parents give you a certain amount of pocket money per week, but you feel this is not enough and not as much as many of your friends get. What do you do?
   - go on strike
   - nick some from Mum/Dad when they're not looking
   - try to reason with them, but accept their decision
   - just accept the situation and don't give them any bother

27   Mr Dunamight

Perhaps foolishly, we sometimes refer to the young people who attend Dunamis as Dunamites, and thus the idea for a strong-person competition was born!

Taking care to include the females who wanted to participate, we staged three tests.

Firstly, we filled a five-gallon water carrier with water, and invited the youngsters to lift it onto a table. Those who were able to do this went through to the next round.

Secondly, we poured half the water out of the container, and gave each competitor 30 seconds to raise the container to shoulder height as often as they could. The counting was strict, and everyone who managed the task more than 20 times went through to the final round.

The final was a thoroughly enjoyable event for all, except me, since the rules demanded that each competitor arm-wrestled with me. The time it took for me to slam their hand to the deck was taken (often it was a very short contest, he said with total dignity and pride), and this was multiplied by their score achieved in the second round. This meant that a winner emerged, and that my arm ached for days afterwards. Excellent fun!

28 Tin-Can Alley

This is a simple indoor game which uses used fizzy drink cans arranged in pyramids, and the vigorous flinging of tennis balls. The rest you can guess. Mind the windows.

29 Table Football
Penalty Shoot-Out

Why use table football just for table football? Be really silly and have a miniature penalty competition, with strikers versus goalies. Whip up support, create an atmosphere, be strongly partisan and have a great time!

30 The Gift Exchange Game

Best played at Christmas time, this is a brilliant way for the young people to give gifts to one another, without anyone being excluded, and it's also wonderful fun. All participants are invited to go out before the day and spend up to £1.50 (not more) on a gift. Each person must wrap the gift and bring it with them on the day of the event. Every person who brings a gift is given a number, which will indicate their turn in the system. The gifts are placed in the centre of the circle of chairs, and the first person has the choice of any of the unopened gifts. They open their gift; let's say it's a biro. (All together, now: "It's a biro!")

The second person now has a choice: they may take the biro from the first person or open another gift. If they take the biro, the person from whom they take it may open another gift of their choice. The third person can choose either of the two opened presents or one of the unopened ones. If they decide to take the biro, say, the person who had the biro then has the same choice – a new unopened present or any of the opened ones, except the present just taken from him or her.

This goes on until the last person has the choice of all the presents: the last unopened one, or any of the others that are now revealed. Very attractive gifts are pinched (sorry, exchanged) several times before the final person has their turn; nothing is safe until the game is over. There will be ample opportunity afterwards to discuss such important topics as materialism, the feeling that things "belong" to us, the joy of giving and so on. A good aspect of this event is that everyone goes home with something.

The first time I played this, I managed to spoil a friend's evening by wrapping up a tin of prunes and a twin pack of toilet paper. One friend could not resist taking it, since the parcel was by far the biggest. Lessons were learned!

31 Treasure Hunt

The forerunner to the Great Dunamis Spycatcher Caper (idea 38), this is energetic and competitive, while it can be as mind-stretching as you like. Clues direct groups of young people to various places, ending up with a treasure of some sort. Good for teamwork, thinking and exercise.

32 Picture Quiz

Taking magazines and butchering them for all kinds of reasons was commonplace in my home while I was growing up, and this idea and the Advert Quiz are two of the reasons we did it so much. Cut out photos of the famous and remove the captions, and this becomes a picture quiz very quickly. A good numbering system, some wall space on which to display the pictures, and plenty of paper and pencils for the young people to write their answers down, and there you have it – 20 minutes of good fun.

It is interesting to see how youngsters help one another, even though they are in competition with one another.

33 Advert Quiz

These days there are some adverts which rely on our product knowledge, but more often than not, the brand names are made clear. Cut adverts out of magazines, and cut the brand names off the adverts. Pin up what remains and award points to everyone who successfully identifies the products. It is always fun to have several rival products, to cause confusion.

34 Not the Pancake Day

A great excuse to have pancakes whenever you want them! Since we were able to use the church kitchen for this, we generated vast flagons of batter, threw grease into red-hot frying pans and everyone made pancakes, with lashings of lemon juice and sugar. Blue smoke filled the room, and several attempts came to a sticky end, but in general a good time was had, albeit an unhealthy one.

35 Giant Pictionary

Pictionary is much the same as charades, except that instead of miming the answer, you have to draw pictures – no writing or talking are allowed, and teams have one minute to decipher the drawing. Giant Pictionary is much the same as Pictionary, except you draw on a large piece of paper for all to see.

If you have never played Pictionary, you clearly don't go to the right sort of party. Go out and live a little!

36 Not the New Year's Eve Party

This took place on New Year's Eve (as you might expect), but we had one problem. How could we occupy all the young people until midnight, and then have a celebration? It would be past 1 a.m. before they could get home, and it would be irresponsible of us to do this. So we did the only thing we could.

Everyone arrived at 6.30 p.m. as usual, but within the confines of our church building, Official Dunamis Time was 9.45 p.m. Constant reference was made to Official Dunamis Time, using a huge clock rigged up for the purpose, and when the clock reached midnight ODT (8.45 p.m. GMT), we welcomed the New Year (I think it was actually a new decade, so we went really mad.)

The cunning part of the scheme was that when we'd had a party for a few minutes, it was still only 9 p.m., our usual finishing time, outside the building. If parents than wished to allow their offspring to stay up until the real midnight, that was up to them, but we'd had our fun earlier on.

Brainwave or what?

37 Completely Silly Games

There comes a time in every youth group when even the perennial favourites like football and rounders become boring, so give them some zip with creative new rules.

Footballoon is excellent fun, if a little slower than what you may be used to – footballers need to demonstrate serious control when running with a balloon, and there are no such things as powerful shots in this game. Crunching tackles often leave the players needing a new balloon, which can be amusing.

Ping Pong Volleyball requires a good eye, painstaking attention and pin-point accuracy. It may also need a supply of balls, since they can be trodden on a bit more often...

Indoor Cricket with a rugby ball allows for very low scores, very few catches and lots of laughs.

OUTSIDE EVENTS REQUIRING A BIT MORE PREPARATION

It is certainly worth a bit of extra effort to make sure that a good time is had by all.

When things are adequately planned, time can be given to getting games and activities properly prepared. Some of these ideas will take a while to arrange, while others are more straightforward.

38 The Great Spy-Catcher Caper

This was a brilliant title for an event which was just as brilliant!

Working with another team member, I took a long walk over the South Downs. We walked from a local windmill, down a hill, along a country lane, through a village, across a few fields, past a boarding school and into another village. As we went, we wrote questions relating to things we passed and invented cryptic clues about the directions we had taken.

When we staged the actual event, a few days later, we took mini-bus loads of young people (supervised by adults) to the windmill, and sent them off with their instructions and a help envelope.

Teams could score 10 points for each right answer to the questions, plus a bonus of 250 points if they arrived at the destination without having to open the help envelope. This contained non-cryptic directions to places of safety, and also gave a telephone number which was manned throughout the time of the game, in case of serious accident or injury. Thankfully, no one has ever had to open their help envelope, but taking safety precautions is always wise.

No points were given for following the directions, since if they took the wrong route, they would not be able to answer any more questions accurately.

The event is not unlike a treasure hunt, except that we have a high expectation that the young people are able to follow a map and therefore orienteering instructions can also be used.

I spent the time of the event (it lasted about 6 hours) driving along country lanes in the church minibus, making sure no team was going in the wrong direction, and giving helpful comments about timekeeping and so on. I also spent a lot of time that day waiting for groups of young people to arrive at various checkpoints. As leaders, we learned some things that day about how long it takes a group of 11-14s to walk a short distance!

Subsequent Spycatcher Capers have been on a much more local scale. Spycatcher Two was a walk from a local park to the church building; Three was an entirely indoor event, which was really just a quiz; and Four was outside again, but this time in a howling, freezing gale along Brighton seafront in the Easter holidays.

This event takes a great deal of preparation, and considerable effort, but it does wonders for encouraging young people to work together as a team, to exercise their bodies and their minds, gives them an extended time in the company of our youth leaders, as well as (at least in the case of the original event) wonderful memories of wading through some nasty mud and being late back for supper, and, doubtless, many other advantages.

By the way, the title was inspired by the trial which surrounded the publication of the book of the same name. It just appealed as something with an air of mystery and a topical feel.

39 The Great Dunamis Chip Shop Survey

It may be my undoing, but I love chips, and am constantly searching for the perfect specimen. This gave the idea for the Dunamis survey of local chip shops. We wrote a list of all the chippies we could remember, and divided the young people into groups so that we could cover as many shops as possible in one hour, with each group responsible for about half a dozen shops.

The young people were armed with a comprehensive form, and when the group had purchased one regular-sized portion of chips from the shop, each individual noted down price, value, and gave a rating for temperature, greasiness versus crispness, quantity, size of chip, wrappings, speed of service, cleanliness of the shop, and so on. Since each person had to reach his or her own conclusions, disagreement was reduced to a minimum of importance in the survey. We included burger and kebab outlets where appropriate, since a chip is a chip (unless it's a french fry, but we still counted them). The results were calculated and the result announced to the young people. Our plan was that the winning shop was to be given a small certificate to commemorate the event, but sadly we never seemed to get around to doing this, since there was the next amazing project to arrange.

There may be someone who doesn't live in a town with a wide range of fast-food outlets; why not have a survey of the chips made by your young people's mothers? The Home-Made Chip Survey, walking from home to home. Or have a Lumpy Custard Event, or a Home-Bred Bread with Street Cred Survey. Imagination rules, OK!

40 The Great Dunamis Triple Thick Shake Survey

We live in a town with many outlets for triple thick shakes. This time the categories under scrutiny were: number of varieties on offer, viscosity (thickness), flavour, temperature, endurance of straw, quality of beaker, speed of service, cleanliness of shop.

41 Wide Games

Many people know different wide games, but these three have worked well, and could probably be improved upon with ease.

A kind of war game (Needs a large park or piece of heathland.) Every participant wears a piece of wool tied around his or her upper arm, with different colours to denote two different "armies". The object of the game is for one army to invade the opposition's camp, where some treasure is stored (use drink cans or something), to steal the treasure and return it to their own camp, while the opposition try to do the same to them. Obviously, strategy demands attackers and defenders on each side, with scuffles and battles going on all over as attempts are made to forcibly remove the wool from each other's arms. Any person who has the wool removed from their arm is unable to continue until they report to the "field hospital", where more wool is issued. This game is good for physical exercise, and helps young people learn tactics and planning.

A damper version (Best played on two sides of a valley.) All young people have a piece of wool on their arm, and they are divided into groups; in turn, each group attempts to steal treasure from an encampment of leaders, who are armed with copious quantities of water. This dissuades a few, but many young people are quite prepared to get wet, and they need to be physically restrained so that their wool can be removed. In this version, once your wool is off, you are out, and have to make way for the wave of attackers.

Four-way football (Needs only an area of grass large enough – it depends on the number of players.) Set up four goals (one on each touchline). Have four teams each with a ball. When the whistle blows, each team attempts to score a goal in any of the other goals, and defends their own goal. When each ball has been used to score a goal, each team returns to its own goal area with a ball and the whistle blows again. Played over a ten-minute period, many goals are scored. The idea of the game is that three teams will gang up on one of the others. Clearly, a strategy of alliance will briefly emerge, only to be laid aside later when the harsh lessons of treachery come into their own!!!

NOT FOR
THE VERY YOUNG

We have discovered that treating young people like adults often brings out the best in them. In some cases it can result in abuse of privileges, and we have to withdraw privileges and treat them with a firmer hand. But one of our most successful moves was to recognise that the older ones in our youth group, those in the 3rd and 4th years at school, did not always appreciate being lumped together with 11- and 12-year-olds.

Thus was born the idea of *Mellow Moments*, an extra hour exclusively for 3rd and 4th years, when they have the opportunity to use the facilities without lots of younger folk getting in their way, and where we address issues more suitable to the level of maturity they have reached.

42 Cafe Paris du Jazz Gentil

Due to an oversight, this was once advertised complete with a spelling error, which made it appear that this event was for non-Jews only! But I digress.

We are blessed at Clarendon Church with a good number of quality musicians, and encouraging some to provide laid-back, relaxing jazz music was not a difficult task. While the musicians entertained, we dressed as waiters with Charlie Chaplin moustaches, moved among the young people who were seated at cafe tables, and served French bread and cheese, with coffee. Some danced gently, while others chatted in franglais, complete with fake accents. It was wonderful.

I realise that not every youth group can call upon gifted musicians, so why not adapt this idea using a tape deck and a collection of suitable tapes? There may well be a "closet jazzer" among your church members, who would be willing and able to suggest some exciting music for the occasion. I think you would do well to have the real sounds of the *Hot Club of Paris*, with Django Reinhardt and Stephane Grappelli.

43 Money
Makes the World Go Around

A series of two seminars, aimed at those who earn wages from Saturday jobs and paper rounds. We discussed budgeting, and the relative wealth of teenagers who have few responsibilities, and, in the second session, addressed the whole area of giving, tithing and generosity. Which good causes should Christians support? What constitutes a good cause? Are we restricted to a rigid 10%? How can we give without pride? What is *hilarious* giving?

Good points were made, and the young people appreciated the help we were able to give them in an informal, non-preachy style.

44 The Video Question

This was the title of one of our occasional debates. We invited two young people to prepare speeches in favour of videos, while two others made themselves ready to oppose the idea. Subjects raised covered all aspects, from the money-making side of video rental, to the dangers of video nasties. Is it right for people to make decisions for us and to censor? Is there any value in the new "12" certificate, if it allows films to show nakedness and sexually explicit scenes? What is the Christian response to a film which uses foul language? Do we need to define the term "foul language" anyway? And what about the disappointing quality of many "Christian" films? Minds were stimulated, and various opinions were expressed.

We found we had to be prepared to let some comments go, while we corrected others and brought Biblical perspective to the discussion. It was helpful to encourage the young people to show courtesy to those expressing opinions which differed from their own. Democracy may not be perfect, but it is needed in a discussion of this nature. "I disapprove of what you say, but I will defend to the death your right to say it" (Voltaire). Cultured, huh?

45 Do Animals Have Rights?

Another debate: this provoked heated but articulate comment from the "bean and pulse" element of our group, while the committed meat-eaters defended themselves magnificently. Gratitude to God for the good things the earth has to offer and responsible attitudes towards living creatures were issues raised in this exciting 30-minute event.

46 *Stand Up for Your Love Rights – What Love Rights?*

The title was suggested by a single released by *Yazoo* around the time. It concerned us that young people were facing puberty and beyond with very little awareness of Christian ethics and morality, except for a vague "don't do it".

We took three sessions. The first looked at the word "love", and pointed out the importance of loving unconditionally, not as the world loves. We are called to have a godly kind of love, "love in spite of". This, sadly, was revelation to some of the young people, but they realised they needed to understand what love was all about.

The second session dealt with the whole vexed question "How far is too far?" and some of the windows became rather steamed up! Being frank and direct is the best way, since it avoids confusion, of which there is already plenty, and it does away with unhelpful sniggering and childish embarrassment very quickly.

The third session was even more direct, as we separated the men from the women for the talk, and female team members spoke to the women about beauty of character being more important than external appearance, while male team members spoke to the men about dealing with lustful thoughts and habits. Again, directness was vital.

47 Indoor Wide Game in the Dark

This was similar to the battling wide game which normally takes place in daylight out of doors. Being in the dark meant there was an element of surprise added to the element of robust enthusiasm. The best fun of all was had by a huge pile of young people rolling in slow motion down the narrow staircase, all desperately struggling to remove wool from each other's arms, retain their own wool, or get someone's foot out of their personal space.

48 Indoor Wide Game with the Lights On

A return to childhood, as half the young people have 90 seconds in which to secrete themselves in the church building, and the others have to find them. When everyone was found, the time taken was noted, and the roles were reversed. Silly, but fun because it was on so huge a scale.

49 Looking at the Body

This was another of our short series; not quite the same as *Stand Up for your Love Rights*, but some of the same material was covered, because it was a little later, and it only takes two years for the members of *Mellow Moments* to graduate to the next age group.

The first session was a discussion on health foods, fad diets and personal health. We discussed some facts about the calorific difference between a can of coke and a can of diet coke, and mention was also made of taste differences. The F-plan, Rosemary Conley and starvation all held our attention for a while, and several helpful points were made about how God requires that we look after ourselves, and avoid over-indulgence in food and in dieting.

The second session covered aspects of physical attractiveness, and the knock-on effect of seeing someone who attracts you. Issues of flirting and dressing to thrill were brought out, and the young people became aware of how much influence they can have over members of the opposite sex. Matters of conduct and clothing were discussed, since a worldly approach is destructive and unhelpful.

50 Your Local Church: How & Why?

Dunamis is rooted in a local church (Clarendon Church, Hove), which has existed in its present form for just over 10 years. We explored some of the reasons for the growth and expansion of the local church, and the reasons why we feel so strongly about church life. We looked at such issues as the exercise of spiritual gifts, eldership, evangelism and growth. It was excellent to have one of the church founder-members and elders with us that evening (Terry Virgo), since he was able to speak with passion and excitement about the work God was building in the area.

51 Quiz the Church Leader

The youth work in Clarendon Church is overseen by one of the elders, and he was invited to take part in an interview and discussion session. This revealed his role in Dunamis, his management position in relation to the leaders of the youth group, his personal vision for youth work and his background.

We also asked him about his preference in triple-decker sandwiches, and his likes and dislikes in the world of pop music, fashion and TV programmes. We felt it brought him into positive contact with the young people, and gave them insights into the life and work of an elder of the church – not an ivory-tower-dweller, but flesh and blood, just like us, except he is anointed by God for a ministry.

52 Environ or Mental?

Another of our formal debates, with young people assigned to speak for and to second the motion that *protecting the global environment is God's perfect will for all Christians,* while others opposed the motion.

The discussion included such points as the command to subdue the earth, the duty to work on the earth, the new earth, any other important things we should do with our time, the rights and wrongs of animal rights protesters, lead-free petrol, government activity, the seal cull, pollution, etc.

It was stimulating intellectually, gave many people the chance to air their views, and could have gone on much longer.

53 Popcorn & Pepsi on the Pier

I am constantly glad that I live on the coast, and in a resort with the excellent facilities of Brighton. I often have a good time on the dodgems, and enjoy the fresh air and opportunities for relaxation afforded by the coastal scenery. But there is also the Palace Pier, which has a huge amusement arcade, deckchairs, funfair rides and stalls selling all the junk food you can imagine.

Taking a crowd of young people with us onto the pier was a great way to pass time, maintaining control over the amount of money they were spending, and on which machines; but enjoying ourselves together socially was excellent for building relationships.

I realise that not everyone lives within easy reach of a pier or an amusement arcade where they would feel it was safe to take their youth group. But many towns (and even villages) have a local gathering spot for young people, and this activity is all about getting youth leaders and team members involved in the lives of the young people, mixing in with them on their territory.

FAMILY EVENINGS

I went on a course run by the local secular youth work department, and they were astonished that Dunamis attempted Family Evenings. We feel that since many of our young people are from church families, we should give parents an insight into the way we run Dunamis, and not just rely on the slightly formal setting of a report during a church council meeting or family evening or whatever.

We also have a burden to influence the parents and relatives of the young people in Dunamis who may never darken the portals of a church, but would be prepared to support their youngsters by coming to the Family Evening. We have attempted several formats for the evening, but have settled for something which contains the elements of: food (coffee & cake, or something more substantial); the Dunawards (jokey prize-giving, packed with in-jokes and fun); a very brief talk; and some activities for parents to join in with their youngsters. We have incorporated a worship time on some occasions, as well.

54 The Great Trivia Quiz

This Family Evening was a success. We arranged each room available to us thematically, and family teams moved from room to room, where team members were posted, armed with questions, some of which were unashamedly culled from the cards in our Junior Edition of Trivial Pursuit.

The themes were: sport, pop music, entertainment, nature, history and geography, and teams which scored the most were given prizes at the end of the evening. It was great to see parents entering in to the fun and competitiveness, relying on their offspring for answers to pop questions, and showing off their historical or geographical prowess (or lack of it).

55 Gatecrashers Anonymous

We ran out of brilliant ideas, so we had the best one of all: what about just having Dunamis as usual, but issue tickets to parents, so that they could gatecrash the event, and join in the fun? Having three times the usual number of people in the building stretched our facilities somewhat, but eight-a-side football with Dads hacking each other's ankles was hilarious.

56 Barn Dance

Employing a professional caller and his band, we staged a really great fun evening for families. This required very little preparation from ourselves, but we were rather at the mercy of the caller, who sometimes said things we would not have felt appropriate or particularly helpful. Never mind, people made allowances for this. Provide plenty of liquid refreshment, preferably chilled.

57 The Dunamis
Double Decathlon

Not ten, but twenty amazing events for family teams to complete, with a typically generous points system. The first ten of these are the same as those described in the Dunamis Decathlon – as the famous England cricketer Mike Smith used to say "play the easy ball!" Anyway, you get my drift, huh? The events:

1. **Soccer Ball Control**
2. **Upstairs, Downstairs**
3. **Basket Shooting**
4. **Estimate a Minute**
5. **Clothes Pegs**
6. **Memory Test**
7. **Hop It**
8. **Balls in a Bucket**
9. **Skip it**
10. **Knocking Down Cans**
11. **Peas and Straws.** Competitors have two plastic tubs: one contains up to 30 dried peas, and the other is empty. Using a straw, with their hands tied behind their back, they must suck up peas and transfer them from one tub to the other. Two points are awarded for each pea in the receiving tub after one minute.
12. **The Cushion Endurance Test.** Competitors stand with their arms stretched out in front of them, at shoulder level, and a pillow is placed on their arms. One point for each second they can keep their arms at the required height, up to a minute.
13. **Penalties.** With the youth group's best goalkeeper between the uprights, competitors can earn 25 points for scoring five goals out of five penalty kicks. They score fifteen points for four goals, ten for three, five for two and two for one (and one for all!).
14. **Get Hammered.** Using a piece of stout hardwood, and a six-inch nail, competitors start with twenty points, and lose three points for each blow of a hammer after the first one needed to drive the head of the nail right into the wood. For safety's sake, a trained, responsible adult should knock the nail into the wood, so that it stands upright of its own accord, and no one need risk their fingers holding it while unskilled youths pretend to be Arnold

Schwarznegger — but they usually turn out to be more like Mr Puniverse.

15.**Reading Shakespeare.** Culture, culture. Each competitor is given a copy of Hamlet's *To be or not to be* soliloquy, and they have to read it aloud as quickly as they are able. They score two points for each second less than 60, no points for slowcoaches, drama, emotion, hand gestures or artistic impression.

16.**Balancing the Books.** Take a collection of hymn books (preferably old ones which are not too precious), and invite each competitor to walk ten yards with a book on his head. Then add another book and let them try again, and award three points for each book carried successfully over the whole of the ten-metre course. This means that if they fail when trying eight books, their score is three times seven books – 21 points.

17.**Puzzle Shapes.** Each competitor has to make geometric shapes from a collection of pieces. Correctly forming a triangle, a square, a rectangle and a circle from the jumbled pieces scores ten points per complete shape. Don't allow more than 60 seconds for this.

18.**Picture Gallery.** Pin up photographs around the building, depicting various famous people (you could use baby photos of the team, if they are well-known to the visiting parents). Award five points for each picture correctly identified.

19.**Word Hunt.** All competitors have all evening to complete a word search incorporating key words to do with the youth group. Three points for each word found.

20.**Write a Limerick.** Give each competitor the same first line to a limerick, and with strict instructions about matters of style, taste and general decorum, invite them to invent the rest of the poem, making it clear that they will be richly rewarded with points for humour, panache, pathos, relevance, honesty, satire and so on. We made it personal by starting with *One evening our friend Andy Back...* but this would not be relevant to your group, so be creative! Have a laugh at someone's expense! Why should it always be me?!

MONEY-RAISING
EVENTS

There are times when cash does not flow as it might, or when special disaster appeals or whatever arise. We have put our creative energy into making sure that our money-raising events have some point and are fun. Sponsored walks are all very well, but achieve little except money-raising and can be very, very boring events in which to take part.

58 The Great Dunamis Car Wash

With buckets, sponges, hoses, washing-up liquid and chamois leathers, we turned the road outside the church building into a car wash for the afternoon, charging a paltry 50p per car. Teams of young people were strongly supervised by team members, and trained in thorough washing techniques, the most important of which is the use of plenty of water, to avoid scratching paintwork.

Part of the morning was spent leafleting the area – placing flyers under the windscreen wipers of each car in the surrounding streets – and this drummed up a lot of business, to supplement the cars of parents of Dunamites.

In one afternoon of frenzied and damp activity, we washed more than thirty cars, and raised a good deal of money – payments and gifts as well.

59 The Beach Clearance

We wrote to the local council, and asked if we would be allowed to collect litter from one of the local beaches, and if so, which beaches should receive our attention. They enthusiastically encouraged us, and so we raised sponsorship. We armed ourselves with black bin bags, fanned out from promenade to shoreline, and collected litter. We filled twelve black sacks, and raised a good deal of money, as well as having an impact on the local environment. It was a lot more fun than it sounds, too!

The great part was that when we sent a photo and press release to the local paper, they included us, which was a free plug for the church youth group. It also showed a level of responsibility, and was good PR for the church. So much so that the national HQ of a big finance company encouraged our clean-up campaign by sending us a cheque for £100! I'm probably not allowed to say which company it was, but our response was "that'll do nicely"!

60 The Amazing Auction

For our fifth birthday, we really went to town and had a massive effort. We scrubbed clean a good number of the church's chairs, with Dunamites gaining sponsors for 30-minute sessions of cleaning. We staged a Dunamis versus Parents football match, with parents required to pay £1 for the privilege, plus Dunamites gaining sponsorship for their performances as well.

But the big event was the auction. For a few weeks, we gathered some amazing items which were given to us to sell at the auction to the highest bidder. We were stunned by the generosity and creativeness of some of the gifts. We amassed watches, clocks, two TVs, lots of confectionery, brassware, crockery, clothing, photographs, knick-knacks and an awful lot of assorted junk as well.

Then parents and well-wishers were invited to bid for items in a hilarious session. A photo of one of the church elders was snapped up for a fiver by an admirer, and several people found themselves paying very generous amounts for things that may not have been worth a great deal.

Perhaps the best idea was to link quality goods with some of the less attractive items as job lots, to try to get rid of the junk. I often enjoy the memory of one generous Dunadad's face when he thought he'd paid seven pounds for a nice little carriage clock, and realised he'd also bought a worn-out tyre for a Ford Escort. He tried to leave it behind at the end, but I spotted him and made sure that we got the best out of the joke!

That evening realised more than £500 as people gave very generously – the purchasers who paid over the odds, and those who gave goods for us to sell. It is a good principle to give away some of the money raised for your own funds, to demonstrate gratitude to God and consistency.

SPIRITUAL
SPECIAL EVENTS

There are times when it is good to make an effort to show that the Godward part of our activities is the reason why we do it, not just to have a great time together or to play games. So we sometimes have a special event which reflects our spiritual values.

61 The Concert

Even using quality Christian bands, concerts are not easy to put on, but can be achieved with a lot of know-how and some effort. They can be a great opportunity for young people to invite their friends, not just to the concert but to the youth group the following week as well. It is important to make sure that the music is as up-to-date as possible, since Christian music has a habit (in the UK, at least) of being slightly behind the times. About 15 years behind in many cases.

We are firmly committed to friendship evangelism, not just in-drag (what Christians often do when we pretend we're doing outreach) of young people for a session when they are "hit with the gospel message", so that they are either converted, or scared off from ever returning. We have found that the proportion of those saved to those inoculated is about one to ten thousand grillion (I exaggerate for effect). It is surely far better to give young people a good youth club that they will want to attend regularly, where they see Christians in action, enter into a time of praise and worship, and receive good, relevant teaching about God and His love for them, than put on such a strong hot-gospel event that we never see them again.

62 The Praise March

It is almost certainly too much to expect your youth group to form the whole of a praise march (where Christians parade through the town with banners, balloons, celebration, dancing and singing), but it is great to encourage them to join in with one in which your church is taking part.

After hearing the reasons for marching through the streets of the town singing and shouting about Jesus, and declaring the good news to passers-by, young people divide into two camps: those who enthusiastically take part in a relatively anonymous form of evangelism with freedom and enthusiasm; and those who become embarrassed to stand up for the name of the Lord.

Having made allowances for the supervision of those who would rather not participate, give the others identity within the march by providing a banner with the youth group name.

What do you mean, your youth group doesn't have a name, as such? Well, give it a name. A name can dramatically improve the corporate identity of the group, making it easier for young people to invite their friends along. Names need to be carefully chosen (not by vote among the young people), since they can reflect the nature of the group.

St Hilda's Young Teens is not ultra-creative, nor desperately attractive, and while *Happ'nin' Crew* may be trendy for a while, it does not say much about what the group stands for or represents.

Names perhaps worthy of consideration may include: *Conquerors; Giantkillers; Mustard Seed; Solid Rock*. I even heard of one group calling itself *The Polo & Whisky Club*, which, being interpreted, meant: Polo is the mint with the hole, and therefore is Holy; and Whisky is a Spirit, thus Holy Spirit. But this was too far-fetched, and attracted the wrong sort of crowd, who said they preferred G&T, and asked when the first chukka was going to get orf.

63 Open Air Evangelism

Again, it may be too ambitious to expect a crowd of young people to stand in a group and sing choruses outside Tesco's, but encouraging them to join in with the church open-air events would be excellent.

Another idea is to arm them with simple questionnaires, and take to the streets, aiming at young people their age, and have conversations which lead to invitations to attend the youth group. Most young people who are excited about being a Christian will participate in this, and find encouragement from the contacts they make.

Above all, let's be realistic about how the young people in our groups take to this idea. Foolishly over-zealous leaders may push them into a kind of exposure for which they are not ready, and they will quickly become discouraged, and put off the idea of standing up for what they believe. But over-cautious avoidance of any contact with unbelievers can be unhelpful, too. Only the Lord knows how strongly to push your group – let Him provoke you into action when the time comes, and exercise great sensitivity and patience.

Being a youth leader isn't meant to be easy!

WORKSHOPS

Each week we promote our workshops, since they often gather a small number of young people who are interested in the activity on offer, and this makes for a good time. I have tried to give the workshops in categories, except for the few miscellaneous items at the end. Workshops are an excellent place for us to make the most of skills and gifting among other church members. Without their help and enthusiasm, we would quickly run out of new things to do.

ART & CRAFT WORKSHOPS

I am grateful to Debbie Jarvis for her invaluable help with this part of the book, since I'm a bit of a sausage-fingers when it comes to the delicate and artistic manoeuvres described here.

64 Card Making

This is great for last-minute presents for Mother's Day or Christmas, and is really quite easy to do. I'm not sure that time should be given to making Valentine cards, since that could put a lot of pressure on younger people in the group for whom this is not such an important event as it is for the older teens.

Wrapping paper can be very well-designed, and it has the added advantage of having the same designs repeated over and over again. Cut motifs from the paper, and mount them on card, taking care to tone the colours, and adding a fancy border. More ambitious cards can be constructed from the same wrapping paper, by building up 3-D designs with a design glued to the card, and then a detail of the design mounted on top, using a sticky-bud, and then another on top of that.

Alternatively, try cutting details of drawings and patterns from other cards and gluing them onto fresh card, with borders and other patterns. The possibilities are endless, and the financial savings enormous!

65 Clay Modelling

The Early Learning Centre can supply plenty of clay for modelling. This can be used in moderately large amounts, and is very inexpensive. The clay dries in the air, so keep it moist until you've finished. The clay also absorbs poster paints well, for finishing your model. Some of the less gifted young people will get a kick out of this activity, since by the end of the evening, they can have something to take away with them which they have made themselves. Encourage the less able and take time with them!

66 Fimo Modelling

Fimo modelling clay is already coloured, can be used for much finer work and is rather more expensive than ordinary clay. It needs to be baked gently in a very low oven (or even one at eye-level, so long as the power's turned right down) and is therefore recommended only for small-scale projects. Using fine tools (such as cocktail sticks or pin-heads) this clay can be sculpted to make attractive creations. Debbie is gifted with this stuff, and shows the young people how to make brooches and badges (with a clasp integrated into the back of the design). The clay can be moulded into initials or flowers or whatever takes your fancy. It can be varnished once it's cooled down from being baked.

I know a woman who claims to be a beginner with Fimo, and she decorated a birthday cake with a model of a young man playing a Hammond Organ, complete with Dr Marten boots and all the accessories which the young man usually carries around with him: sunglasses, sheet music, filofax and so on. And the face was an excellent likeness, too! Recognising the application and patience of some young teens, there must be some middle ground where art and play meet.

67 The DunaMural

Involving a good number of young people, the construction of a mural which depicts many aspects of Dunamis was inventive and fun. We gathered together broken ping-pong balls, busted badminton rackets, thrown-away Mars Bars wrappers and finished-with cans of Coke to form the background to the mural. We added a Dunamis brochure, a woolly hat, a welly, several photocopied worksheets from teaching sessions and a whole load of other items too numerous to mention (or remember) and glued them all on a piece of hardboard in a design which was jumbled, but attractive. Then the whole lot was sprayed gold, using an aerosol (ozone-friendly) or car paint, working outside one sunny afternoon. The mural was displayed at the Family Evening a few weeks later.

An objet d'art? Far from it, but a broad statement of our activities.

68 T-shirt Printing (Make a Statement)

The young people supply an old T-shirt (preferably white), and we supply fabric paints and some stencils with appropriate slogans already cut out. There is much skill required in applying the colours to the shirt through the stencil, and then ironing in the dyes. It is possible to find pens filled with fabric dye, which are easier to control.

The kinds of slogan which may appeal: *Jesus Rules OK*; *Get saved now! (Ask me how)*; *My feet are on the rock, and my name is on the roll – that's why they call it rock & roll.* You may find that some young people prefer to draw, and this gives scope for pictures which reflect aspects of God's creativity – nature, families, sunsets, music, etc.

69 Banner Making

The easiest way to make a convincing banner is to use a technique called appliqué, which involves sewing materials onto other materials. Sounds fun? It is! Use a plain background for the main body of the banner, and cut out letters to spell out the text or phrase you wish to make. It is hard to imagine that young people will have sufficient staying-power to complete the banner, so be prepared to take it home afterwards and finish it off!

Perhaps the best banner made by young people I have ever seen was made of blue felt, and said *Jesus sets us free from conformity*, and all the letters were in white, except for the 'f' in conformity, which made the point beautifully.

With two poles inserted into sleeves sewn up the sides, a banner can be a rallying point for a praise march.

70 Put a Sock in It!

This is a silly name for the making of puppets using old socks. All you need is a sense of humour, the ability to throw your voice, or at least say "Gottle o' Geer", some old plain socks, some felt and some glue.

Using intuition and some flair, stick on bits of felt to represent eyes, nostrils (with or without long dangly matted hairs), a wig, teeth, etc., and then have a puppet show. Come back Kermit the Frog, all is forgiven!

71 Drama: Improvisation

This calls for thinking on your feet, lightening reactions and a quick wit, but can easily be achieved by many young people, because their humour is like that.

Pairs are given situations in which they must work, or the characters they must put on. For example:
- One of you has been handcuffed to a lamp-post, and you must persuade the other one to help set you free.
- One of you has just broken one of the toilets in Buckingham Palace, and the other is a butler who has come to investigate the flooding.
- Both of you can only communicate with gestures and whistles. One must tell the other a joke.
- Both of you are elderly and frail, and you get into an argument.

72 Paint Your Nails

I walked into the room while this workshop was in full swing, and felt sure that the atmosphere was either injurious to health or likely to cause hallucinations. It seems that nail varnish is a powerfully strong substance – I'd never realised this before. Word of advice learned by our experience – fling wide the windows, and get a through draught.

The idea of the workshop is to understand that your hands (strictly speaking, your nails) can be a canvas for creative expression. Rather than just layering a wedge of red varnish on them, why not draw on them? Girls emerged from the workshop with amazingly attractive designs and patterns – stars and dots, etc. – literally at their fingertips.

73 Eggheads

Originally an Easter activity, this workshop develops the idea of painting eggs, and turns it into an artform. Using wool, felt and other materials, hard-boiled eggs are decorated and then painted to look like heads – some bald, but others with woolly wigs and suchlike.

74 Pebble Painting

Since we live on the coast, pebbles are easy to come by. When washed they make interesting paperweights or simple decorations with the use of artists' paints — poster paint is absorbed by the porous stones, and loses its brightness. It also washes off. We use acrylic paints and varnish. Faces, maps, designs, flowers, marbling effects – anything goes. Some people like to stick a piece of felt on the underside of the pebble to prevent scratching, and then present the stone in a little box. They make an attractive and original gift.

CATERING WORKSHOPS

If you have a suitable kitchen, you will doubtless already be
staging catering workshops. But some of these link to a theme,
some require a little more creativity, and some just need plenty of
nerve! Be safe, won't you?

75 Sweet Sensations

As the title suggests, this can be anything with a high calorific
value – either simple, like flapjack, vanilla ice (very trendy at the
moment), or something more ambitious, like meringue nests, or
toffee. Whatever you do, make sure that you have sufficient adults
supervising so that safety is the first thought. Hot toffee could
disfigure someone for life, so treat it with great care, and only
attempt it with the most responsible and aware teens. The same
goes for apple doughnuts (make them about the size of chinese
prawn balls) or anything else deep-fried, since hot oil can be
dangerous if mishandled.

76 Recipe for Disaster

At the risk of being sexist, this is a catering workshop designed for
the unfairer sex. Any person with patience could teach a group of
young men how to make a sausage plait, or even Scotch eggs.
Clearing up after them might require a very great deal of patience,
however.

77 Easter Catering

You guessed it. Anything to do with eggs or chocolate, or chicken or bunnies or buns would be suitable for this. Here are three possible ideas. Melt cooking chocolate in a bowl which sits in a pan of water (bain-marie, actually; I bet you're impressed by my wide-ranging knowledge) and paint it into egg moulds. When it cools, the chocolate can be removed from the mould and decorated with icing sugar and other items too sweet and calorific to be imagined.

Or make Easter bonnet biscuits, with digestives decorated with marshmallows, butter cream, marzipan, and little bits of ribbon. Do not eat the ribbon. Or create your own finger-lickin' breadcrumb mix and coat chicken drumsticks before plunging them (with all safety precautions) into a vat of boiling oil.

78 Through the Year with the Catering Workshop

Since cooking is such a popular activity as a workshop, we have provided one each month, and given it a name which reflects the passing year:

Jammy January	Doughnuts or jam tarts
Flippin' February	Pancakes
Munchy March	Flapjacks or Cornflake Clusters
Apples in April	Apple Amber (meringue topping over apple)
Marshmallows in May	Toasted, over an open fire
Jelly in June	Moulds come into their own
Juicy July	Fruit Flan
Ambitious August	Baked Alaska – go on, have a try; you only live once...
Sweet September	Anything highly calorific
Octopus in October	Octopus-shaped cheese pastry
Nutty November	Cheesecake topped with walnuts
Dunkin' December	Biscuits dipped in chocolate and hundreds and thousands

OFF-SITE WORKSHOPS

It can be helpful to take a small number of young people outside for an activity now and again. It may relieve an over-filled church building, but it does require a higher level of supervision. Have a go – the fresh air will do you good!

79 Ornithology

If there is a large park nearby, you may be able to find a wide variety of feathered friends within a small area. This needs a certain amount of knowledge and skill in recognition.

80 Train Spotting

Brighton is well-served by trains of many varieties, and this makes it an ideal place for donning an anorak and a bobble hat and becoming a wally for a while. But perhaps this would cost your pride or your street-cred too much. Having said that, there must be a way of examining trains and stations which doesn't require such extreme measures.

Many people find the investigation of trains interesting, and you don't have to dress foolishly to do this. Also, consider the possibility of steam railways near your location...

HIGH-ENERGY WORKSHOPS

I have often fallen into the trap of thinking that a workshop must be quiet and concentrated – these are ideas for loud and boisterous ones.

81 When the Going gets Tough

...the tough get going! This is a workshop to test your strength and give you the opportunity for some body-building. This needs some knowledge and experience, or damage to muscles or bones may result, but sounds like too much effort for me! The kinds of activities can range from sit-ups, chin-ups and jogging on the spot, to more punishing routines. It sounds positively dangerous. I prefer the saying that when the going gets tough, the tough go shopping!

82 Dancing

Debbie Jarvis is a very energetic leader, and enjoys teaching young people to dance in formation, like all those people who prance about in between the jokes on bad comedy and variety shows. But young people seem to enjoy it, so I shouldn't knock it, I suppose...

Debbie is convinced that some of the excellent relationships she enjoys with young people who have grown up through Dunamis are due in part to the bonding which takes place when working together on creative projects such as designing and choreographing a dance. She often uses Christian music, too, which exposes the young people to positive lyrics, rather than choosing something less wholesome.

83 Aerobics

This is getting silly. The least energetic way to do this is to encourage the young people to dance along with the *Jane Fonda Video Workout*. Doubtless this is good for fitness and health.

WORKSHOPS HARD TO CATEGORISE

Please note the long-winded avoidance of the word "Miscellaneous". It would have been too easy.

84 The Dunavid

I went on a brilliant holiday with two friends a couple of years ago, and we decided to hire a camcorder from a high street rental agency, and make our own video. With a bit of creativity, and a few camera techniques, we had a great laugh. The idea occurred to me that we might be able to do the same kind of thing with the young people.

We had two sessions: the first was all about lighting and camera angles, panning and dollying, focusing and depth of field. This was deliberately technical, but many of the young people cottoned on. The second session was the making of the video itself, with several young people larking about and being extremely silly, which was amusing, and holding up written messages for their mums, which were amazing. We then filmed a sequence at the start of one of our Power Hours, which was fun to do.

The finished result was, of course, unedited, and went on for rather a long time. It wasn't all that interesting to watch, since the light levels were poor, and none of us is Franco Zefferelli, and none of us is that good an actor. We would certainly do better the next time, by attempting something less ambitious. You have to try these things in order to discover if there is a budding Tom Cruise or Michelle Pfeiffer in your ranks.

85 First Aid

Yawn city, I hear you cry. But when you have someone with an understanding of first aid and a sense of humour, the workshop can become excellent fun. A few well-chosen words about wounds, bandages, the recovery position and shock were followed by a demonstration of how to deal with someone who has been involved in an accident. One of the young people volunteered to pretend to be the victim, and the others set about him with bandages, sticky plaster and wild abandon. The victim finished up looking like the star part from *The Mummy's Curse Meets the Invisible Man*! The intention was that each person was practising their first aid on a different part of the victim, but all put together, it was a dynamic result.

It is important to avoid actually giving someone the kiss of life if they are breathing normally.

86 Music Making

There is a growing interest in ethnic music among young people, and this inspired us to do a music making workshop for the musically inept. Raiding the condiment shelves of our store cupboards, we came up with shakers, rattlers, things to hit and things to hit with, and formed our own Latin Salsa Groove Reggae Cajun Folk Hip Hop Creole Band for the evening. A little accompanying bass and piano, and we were off, moving to a seriously rhythmical wall of sound. True, it wasn't music, but so what?

87 Radio-Controlled Cars

We asked our young people how many of them had radio-controlled cars, and, to our amazement, several indicated that they had such items. They all brought them in one evening, and there were races and stunts going on to the amusement of many. Simple, but fun.

88 Computers

We had two young people in the group who were prepared to bring in their PCP's and many young people had a great time playing shoot-'em-ups and suchlike. Since the machines were theirs, they supervised the others.

This was a better arrangement than what had happened before, with one of our team kindly bringing in his BBC. He understandably guarded it all evening, tying him up with a very few young people, when we could have used his presence elsewhere in the building. This may be fine if you have a small youth group, but when we have 85 young people, and only 10 or 12 team members, we cannot afford the luxury of supervision at this ratio.

89 *Top of the Pops* Video

This is similar to the Pop Panel, but is on a smaller scale. It is simply a rerun of a recent TOTP, giving young people opportunity to fast forward or stop and discuss.

We asked questions about the quality, meaning and style of the songs – do they promote godliness, worldliness or something worse? What about the presenters – why do they shout, and is it a good idea to have people who are known as children's TV stars promoting songs which are more geared towards young adults? Blue Peter presenters should perhaps not be seen to be promoting songs with strong sexual content.

What about the style of the videos? Do they tell a story, project images, help the song, redeem an otherwise bad song, or what? Is this good or bad? Why? What about the quality of the chart overall? Is there a tendency towards one kind of music or a wide variety? What does this suggest? Where have all the teeny-boppers gone? Do you think the appeal of pop stars is aimed at younger and younger audiences? Is this okay? Where are the important songs and singers who bring art and youth culture together? And please do something about the intro music to EastEnders, which is surely due for a change. Thank you.

90 Fashion

Play a recent video of *The Clothes Show* or *Frocks on the Box* and discuss the fashions. Perhaps a five-minute piece about the importance of things which do not change would be helpful, stressing the fun and excitement of fashion alongside its expense and fickleness.

Alternatively, it can be fun to have a fashion competition, by giving young people three bin bags, three insides of toilet rolls, three long strips of toilet paper, crepe paper, coloured sheets of paper, sellotape and staplers, and 30 minutes in which to create an outfit, plus hat, plus other accessories, all worn over their clothes. They then parade around the room at the start of the meeting, with a *clapometer* style of marking from their peers.

Workshops like this can give plenty of opportunity to make a few comments about the importance of inner beauty as well as making the most of your appearance.

91 The Dynamic DunaDog Demo

Two church members have trained their dogs to the point where they take part in competitions – not to judge their beauty or pedigree, but to test them at retrieving various things, obedience, jumping and other tricks.

We set up chairs along the length of the hall, and the two dogs and their handlers impressed us all. A gun was fired, and the dogs didn't flinch, but many of our young people were visibly shaken. The dogs climbed, jumped, retrieved and were more obedient than anyone thought possible.

My reason for including this highly specific workshop, which is not the sort of thing everyone could do, is to stimulate you into thinking about church members you know who may be able to amuse or amaze the young people in your group. Jugglers, fireaters, conjurers, musicians, artists... However, please make sure not only that the subject matter is suitable for young people, but also that the expert is able to communicate some of their excitement and authority to the young people while they share their talents. For example, rustic Jack Hargreaves characters talking to city street kids about whittlin', ploughin' and tyin' your own late-risin' flies may be out of their depth.

OUT-OF-HOURS
EVENTS

Our experience tells us that when we spend quality time with our young people, there is a positive effect on them. So we make a point of including some all-day events on our programme, which are demanding of the team, but worthwhile.

92 Local Places of Interest

Dullsville, man, I hear you cry. I agree, if you go where school trips go – Roman Villas, Museums, archaeological digs – not that these places are necessarily boring, but that they are sometimes associated with boring teaching methods. Why not see if there are more exciting places to visit? A sweet factory, or a steelworks. Even a coal mine. It may be that you have friends who work in these industries, and you may be able to persuade them. The youth group can often boldly go where no school party has been before, simply because a higher level of discipline, or a smaller group can be arranged. If they say "no way José" you've lost nothing, but if they say "OK", you're in like Riley, aren't you?

93 Ice Skating

Our annual pilgrimage to Slough Ice Rink (yes, Slough, all the way from Brighton) is immensely popular. It's a dangerous and painful sport but hilarious, especially if there are people in your group who are prepared to fall down at regular intervals for the amusement of all.

94 Swimming

If you are able to book the baths for your exclusive use, you can play water polo, or take all manner of floating things with you. There is an issue here, however; we emphasise the importance of respecting one another in the way we dress, and there is no point in placing young people in the path of temptation.

Having said this, we sometimes take our group swimming on Sunday mornings, to ring the changes for them – if life becomes predictable, then it is in danger of being boring; but variety is the spice...

95 Mystery Tour

The last time we had a day out, the bus driver got lost, and we had our very own home-made mystery tour on our hands. But a better way to arrange things is to decide on a good place to go to, and then not tell anyone. This has the added advantage that you don't have to decide where you are going to until quite near the date – a cunning scheme which we have had to employ many times at Dunamis, although it's never my fault...

But the key point is to make sure that the place you finish up is interesting or fun, or your mystery will turn into a disappointment.

96 Dunapicnics

Summer Sundays can be an excellent opportunity for introducing parents to the joys of some of the activities I've already mentioned, especially the ones where the young people will have every chance of winning convincingly. Simply taking a group of young people out for a picnic in a park would be an enjoyable afternoon.

Better than sitting at home watching some old black and white film on BBC2.

97 Five-a-side
in Local Sports Centre

Instead of just playing football in a park or inside our regular meeting-place, we sometimes make the effort of hiring the local sports hall, and playing on a purpose-built 5-a-side court, complete with goals and nets. It is expensive but worth it. There is also an all-weather surface in one of the nearby parks, which can be hired for football during the winter (it reverts to tennis during the summer months). The variety is worth the expense, and you can always charge £1 per head for the privilege of playing...

98 It's a Knockout (versus Parents)

Do you remember those dreadful Friday evenings, when you balanced a plate of fish, chips, peas and piccalilli on your lap as Stuart Hall and Eddie Waring laughed maniacally at you from Great Yarmouth or even Marseilles on *Jeux Sans Frontières,* and students and bank clerks who were old enough to know better played the joker or went to pieces on the mini-marathon? You do?

Re-live those painful memories in the comfort of your own local park as young people and their parents prance about.

1. **The Wet One.** One team ferries water from one end of a 20-metre course to the other using buckets, while all the other teams bombard them with footballs. Those carrying water can return for more bucketfuls, and they have two minutes to get as much water as they can into the collecting bin at the end of the course. They may prefer to soak their opponents, of course. Water successfully transferred is measured and the team which collects the most is declared the winner.

2. **Quick Change Relay.** Each member of the team dons some enormous and cumbersome clothing before running 50 metres, where they remove the clothing, so that another team member can put it on and run back again, and so on until everyone has run the course.

3. **The Blindfolded Obstacle Course.** Blindfold the whole team, and one by one they take on a difficult obstacle course. Please make sure that there are plenty of things to trip over, as well as lots of water on the grass where they will fall. Be as fiendish as possible!

4. **Crab Football.** Using a small patch of dry grass, set up goals, and play football, except all players have to move about by supporting themselves on their hands and feet, tummies towards the heavens. This is truly exhausting!

5. **The Damp Balance.** Combatants stand on a plank suspended between chairs, and attempt to knock each other off using soft implements, such as pillows. Meanwhile, other players hose them with water. This is not recommended for use during droughts or while hosepipe bans are in force.

LONGER EVENTS

The spiritual advantages of weekends away or even week-long holidays are enormous, as young people are given the opportunity to focus their attention on their relationship with God, are kept slightly away from the more severe temptations which may assail them at school or at home, and they spend time in the company of your team of youth workers. These events are hard to organise, require significant sacrifice of time on the part of your team, but pay enormous dividends.

99 All-Day Dunamis

We started with a cooked breakfast at 9 a.m., and staged competitions and extra games all day. The afternoon was given over to an *It's a Knockout* competition, and then at 6.30 p.m., regular Dunamis started, with those who were not present all day joining in. The Power Hour that day was electric.

100 Stayovers

A simple overnight event can be a good introduction to the idea. I believe there is no advantage in having mixed genders in any building where there is only one bathroom available; there are only dangerous disadvantages. It is generally necessary to be very strict about the rules when young people are sharing sleeping accommodation; the reasons are obvious.

101 The Numbers Game

Imaginations were fired when we announced 24-hour Dunamis, from noon Saturday to noon Sunday, the end of the church meeting. Then came 32-hour Dunamis, which ran from 9 a.m. on Saturday until 5 p.m. Sunday, but felt like a week. 48-hour Dunamis saw us in action from 6.30 p.m. Friday night until 6.30 p.m. Sunday.

We were in trouble, then, because there was nowhere else to go except into working hours. Team members were asked to take time off work for 99-hour Dunamis, which started at 9 a.m. on Thursday morning, and finished at noon on Sunday. The sharp ones among you will have spotted that this was only 75 hours, but this was due mainly to a lucky slip when we produced our publicity material, and we should have put "Wednesday".

The programme has now passed into the mists of time, but looked something like this:

Thursday
9 a.m.   Arrive: competitions and championships begin
10.30 a.m. Coffee and make your packed lunch
11 a.m.   Trip out to Littlehampton, (funfair about 25 miles away)
5 p.m.   Return; dinner
6 p.m.   Competitions etc., continue
7.30 p.m.   Meeting: *Session One* – worship, preaching, ministry time, etc.
9.15 p.m.   Video, hot chocolate and biscuits
10.30 p.m. Prepare for bed; impromptu pillow fights etc.
11 p.m.   Lights out (said the programme)
11.15 p.m. Lights out (actually)
12.30 a.m. Silence required

Friday
8.30 a.m.   Breakfast
9.15 a.m.   Competitions continue
9.45 a.m.   Make your packed lunch
10.15 a.m. Leave for local park; football and rounders
11.30 a.m. First team taken for *The Great Spycatcher Caper*
6.30 p.m.   Last team arrives back from *Spycatcher Caper*
6.45 p.m.   Dinner
7.45 p.m.   Meeting: *Session Two* – worship, preaching, ministry etc.
9.15 p.m.   Hot choc, video
10.30 p.m. Bed as before

Saturday
9 a.m.   Breakfast
10 a.m.   The *Dunadecathlon* begins
11 a.m.   Coffee
11.15 a.m. *Decathlon* continues
12.30 p.m. Lunch
2 p.m.   Leave for *Tide Fight*
             (This was not really altogether successful, and has therefore not been included in this book. See, I'm an honest chap.)
4.30 p.m.   Return from *Tide Fight*, competitions continue

5.15 p.m.   Dinner
6 p.m.   Clear up
6.30 p.m.   Dunamis begins as usual, including finals of
           competitions and Meeting: *Session Three* – worship,
           teaching and ministry
9 p.m.   Dunamis ends as usual; *Mellow Moments*
           (for 3rd and 4th years) begins
10 p.m.   *Mellow Moments* ends as usual
10.15 p.m. Quick video, hot choc and biscuits
11 p.m.   Prepare for bed...
1 a.m.   Unofficial feasting (subtly supervised)

Sunday
8.15 a.m. Breakfast
9 a.m.   *The Clear-Up Event of the Year* (dull, but necessary)
10 a.m.   Church meeting begins
12 noon   Church meeting ends and so does 99-hour
           Dunamis...phew!

Then we really paid for it, and had 4444 minute Dunamis, from
6.54 p.m. on Thursday evening, until 9 p.m. Sunday. But no one
realised that this actually only amounted to just over 74 hours.
Sneaky or what?

AFTERWORD

Above all, please make sure that you have as much fun as they have. Most of the trick is to be enthusiastic, and young people will join in and have a good time, and may even learn something about themselves, each other, you, society, God, relationships, reactions, and the world in which they live.

And if young people have a good time at your church youth group, then that alone is excellent news, because it underlines the message to them that being a Christian is not naff but good; it is not gloomy or boring but sparkling and enjoyable; it is far from deadly or old-fashioned but full of life and hope!